Prayers for Teenagers

PRAYERS FOR
TEENAGERS

compiled by
NICK ▲ AIKEN

Marshall Pickering
An Imprint of HarperCollins*Publishers*

Marshall Pickering is an imprint of
HarperCollins*Religious*
Part of HarperCollins*Publishers*
77-85 Fulham Palace Road, London W6 8JB

First published in Great Britain
in 1989 by Marshall Morgan and Scott,
forerunner of Marshall Pickering
3 5 7 9 10 8 6 4

A catalogue record for this book
is available from the British Library

ISBN 0 551 01931 X

Acknowledgement is made to Hodder & Stoughton for
use of material from the Holy Bible, New International
Version 1773, 1978, 1984 International Bible Society

Printed and bound in Great Britain by
HarperCollinsManufacturing, Glasgow

To Mum and Dad, Sharon
and Louise,
with much love and thanks

Contents

PRAYERS FOR

Acknowledgments

I have a vast number of people to thank who have contributed towards this book of prayers for teenagers. I received prayers from young people all over the country, though mainly from teenagers who are members of youth groups from the Guildford Diocese. I would like to thank Martin Hook, Anna Matthews, Melissa Sherwood, Katherine Wilson, Marion Hore, Edward Fraser, Katy Watkins, Helen Askew, David Butcher, Ben Taylor, Anna-Marie Rotheisen, Richard Markwick, Andrew Vincent, Zimba Moore, Gillian Elsmore, Richard Huxley, Julie Guyer, Tanya Lancaster, Natasha Fraser, Julie Arthur, Tammy Harris, Esther Rich, Marguerite Devar..ley, Nicola Woodgate, Rachel Curtis, Nikki King, Charlie Olsen, Alex Barlow, Jane Curtis, Kathrine White, Suzanne Green, Guy Travers, Sally Hawkins, Sophia Moore, Debbie Clark, Vicky Fraser, Emma King, Nick Hyde, Matthew Thomas, Lucy Bouch, Tracy Godwin, Jane Hanson, Katy Watkins, Ned Palfrey, Susanna Martin, Gabrielle Allnutt, Julia Dignan, Jo Cotton, Lucie Brailsford, Karen Willson, Paul Humphrey, Steven Knight, Vicky Searchfield, Colin McCoy, Julia Stevens, Simon Martin, Karen Taylor, Suzanna Earle, Sarah McLogan, Jo Teasdale, Nicki Simmonds, Louise Aiken, Alison Buller, Rachel Fellingham, Katherine Short, Claire Revel, Lucinda Thunhurst, Kirsty Hook, Jo Coward, Sara Wilson, Sarah Warne, Stephanie Edwards, Gavin Bainbridge, Zoe Smale, Sammie Harvey, David Barber,

Lucy Baines, Jill Bowdery, Emma Matthews, Tim Rose, Beverley Polington, Stephen Willson, Claire Morse, Sarah Goodson, Cathy Porter and many whose prayers are included in this book but whose name I don't know.

I hope as you read and use the prayers in this book you will find them of help and an inspiration.

I would also like to thank Ruth Drury, Tammy Harris, Claire Morse, Suzanna Martin, Robert Tobias, Lisa Stubbing, Emma-Jane Ericson, Sonya McAnulla, Stephen McAnulla, Gillian Elsmore, Rachel Curtis, Jane Curtis, Rosie Goddard, Jonathan Beasley, Nick Vincent, Alex Griffin, Natasha Fraser, Tracy Crow, Richard Markwick, Frances Wood, Ned Palfrey and Tanya Lancaster who helped me in choosing the prayers and compiling the book. Their assistance was of immense value and to them I am very grateful.

To my colleagues in the Education Department at Diocesan House I am grateful for all their help and support. In particular I would like to thank Anne Plunkett who laboured in typing the manuscript and who is a patient and excellent secretary.

As you may know all the royalties from this book will go to the work of the Prince's Trust. The Trust does such a valuable and important work among young people in Britain today. It is a privilege to be involved in its work and I hope that the money the book earns will give a lot of valuable help to young people throughout the country.

Finally, may I stress that all the prayers in this book are basically unedited: they are an expression of what the teenagers felt and the way they wanted to articulate it.

NICK AIKEN

Some Helpful Thoughts on How to Pray

Prayer is wonderful. It allows God to look into us and see us. Women and men down the centuries have discovered that prayer is in fact a very crucial part of life. Without prayer, life can be very hard and dry. But when we allow God to look into us and when we look at him then something very powerful happens. It brings us back to life. It puts us in touch with God. So what is prayer all about?

Well let's start with God. It is God who is our Father in heaven. It is he who cares about us — loves us and because he has made us his children it is only right that we should come to him with our thanks and gratitude and requests. After all he created us.

So what does God want us to do — well, to love and worship him. To commit our lives to him and to show that we love him by our words and actions. He wants to change our lives — to make them better. He wants us to be strong and courageous so that what we do we do out of love and trust.

You see prayer brings us right into the presence of God. It is like opening a door which allows you to go inside to this vast throne room where God is present as King and Ruler. Prayer is a privilege. No one would think about bursting into God's presence — rather you should come in gently and reverently remembering who it is you are talking to. Do you remember when Jesus taught the disciples the Lord's Prayer he said we should begin by saying 'Our Father who art in heaven, hallowed be your name . . .' In other words God reigns in heaven as Lord and Ruler and his name is to be honoured and revered. But the wonderful thing is that this great and mighty king actually allows us to come into his presence — he invites us in, to come and sit with him and talk and discuss all that concerns and worries us — actually like a friend.

Well what should we talk to him about. Of course about our concerns, but much more than that. We should talk about him and what he has done for us. There are plenty of things we can thank him for — our life, food, health, parents, friends, family, a job. There will always be something positive, something good that we can find that we should say thank you for. In fact if you really think about it there will be a multitude of things — both great and small that it is worth saying thank you for. You don't have to get carried away with it but just show and express your gratitude.

Have you ever been to a pop concert? Most of you I guess will say yes, and if you have not been then you probably hope to go one day. They are very noisy affairs with lots of energy, lights and enthusiasm. You can almost see the sound of music hit the roof and bounce off. Well that's a little like heaven: the angels' praise and worship hits the roof.

God wants us to worship him sometimes quietly and reverently but sometimes with a loud voice as well. Sometimes we may feel we want to shout his praises from the rooftops, thanking him for all he has done. If you feel that way at times don't ever think it's inappropriate because Psalm 47 says:

> Clap your hands, all peoples!
> Shout to God with loud songs of joy
> For the Lord, the Most High, is terrible,
> a great King over all the earth.

I don't think that heaven is quiet all of the time. In fact I'm sure it is a pretty noisy and exciting place.

It is terribly important that we should express our

gratitude and thanks to God because there is nothing worse than someone who does not show their gratitude and say thank you. It is very rude. You can probably remember the times you have been hurt when someone has not bothered to show their appreciation. Well you can imagine what God feels — so it's important to say thanks.

So what should we do next? Well, pray for others. Pray for your Mum. Pray that God may bless her. If she has had a hard time ask that she may be given strength and courage to do her work. Try and make life easier for her by offering some practical help. Make your bed. Tidy your room. Ease the hassle that makes things difficult at times.

Pray for your Dad. Maybe things have been difficult at work with various pressures. It's not easy at work. Work can involve a lot of stress because of all the various responsibilities involved. Pray for Dad. Pray that your relationship with him may improve and grow stronger. Dads as well as Mums are very special so they deserve our prayers. You may not get on very well with your parents at times and things may be pretty bad at home. But prayer can help. It can help you see your parents in a better light. It can help you understand what they feel. It is actually not easy being a parent. It's hard work and sometimes *you* don't make it any easier. So show your love and care and ask God to bless your family.

Then what about your friends and their ups and downs? It's great to have friends. In fact friends are absolutely crucial. Just think where you would be without them — sometimes you might think better off! Friends can irritate you and get you down but actually we all know that we need them. So pray for them. Be kind to them and try and show them your love and care.

Prayer is so important because it strengthens our relationships with our friends. It shows that we are thinking of them and wish that only good shall come their way. Prayer can make a relationship special and it's great to be able to pray for our friends because of the strength and help it can give them.

Prayer is also concerned with saying sorry. Sometimes we do not tell the truth. We are unkind and selfish to others. Well we cannot come into God's presence as if nothing has happened; rather we must ask God to forgive us. It might be an idea to stop for a few moments during your prayers and just recall the things that you know you've done wrong. Maybe you were bad tempered with someone or bitchy behind their backs saying something that was cruel. Maybe your thoughts were filled with sexual ideas which you know were not good. The great thing is that we need not walk around feeling guilty about what we have done wrong because when we ask God to forgive us — he does! He forgives and forgets. No matter what we have done or how bad it is he will forgive us and because he forgives us he wants us to forgive others.

Prayer is also about being quiet at times. Things may be noisy at home so where do you go to be quiet? Well, of course, there is always your bedroom if you are lucky to have one of your own. But sometimes going off for a walk gives the opportunity of being alone to think and pray. In fact Jesus at times just couldn't cope with the vast crowds that followed him and chased after him so he used to go up into the mountain to pray and listen to God.

There may not be too many mountains round where you live but there may be somewhere where you will not be disturbed and where you can be alone with your thoughts. Which reminds me, you do not have to kneel or close your eyes when you pray. In fact prayers can be said anywhere at any time, no matter what you are doing. Maybe it's easier when you are alone and can concentrate but nothing is to stop you saying a prayer when you are walking along the corridor at school or sitting on the bus on the way home.

Someone once said that basically prayer is talking to God. But that's not all there is to it. It is also about listening to God. You may say don't be crazy — how can you listen to God? Only people who are mad claim that God talks to them. Was St Paul crazy or Moses or Abraham? No of course they weren't. God does speak and we should listen. And how do we listen? Simple! Discover what love is all about because God is love and he puts his love in our hearts. So when we do something selfish or wrong it somehow does not feel right. It makes you feel uncomfortable and you don't feel good about it at all. That is God speaking, showing you that love and friendship is greater and stronger than greed and selfishness. Let me put it another way. When we see something beautiful it makes us feel good and it inspires us. God is beautiful. In fact he is more beautiful than any precious stone or diamond ring. He is more beautiful than any snow-capped mountain or lush green valley. So he speaks to us not only through the beauty of all the created things around us but through the friendship of others and the care that he shows us through Jesus his Son. Jesus shows us what God is like. He came to show us what is good and true. So if you want God to speak to you look at all the beautiful things and the things that are so powerful like trust, love, truth, honesty and faith. And most of all look at Jesus because, as I said, he showed us by his words and actions what God is like and what he wants us to do with our lives in this his world.

I don't want to give you a long talk on prayer because prayer is simply talking and listening to God as you would to a friend. But just to recap what I've said and add in a bit more, here are some guidelines about the different approaches to prayer.

The Place
Can be anywhere but best when you are alone.

The Time
Up to you. First thing in the morning or last thing at night. Basically any time you like, but try to make it regular.

Who do you pray to?
God your heavenly Father who loves you and cares about you. He invites you into his presence.

What Do You Say?
Whatever you like. But best to include your thanks and gratitude. Mention your family and friends and mention your requests. Say sorry for what you have done wrong.

Do You Have to Kneel?
No. You can stand or sit. You can pray with your eyes open or closed. It doesn't matter.

How Do I Listen to God?
By knowing the truth of God's love and asking forgiveness when you know you have done wrong.

Does it Work?
The important thing about prayer is not getting God to do things for us but discovering what he wants us to do for him.

Does God Always Answer Prayer?
Yes, but God does not always give the answers we want. He always acts to do what is best for us. We cannot dictate to God what he should do. Remember even Jesus asked God if he could avoid the cross but God said no because through his death he was going to allow the most important event in human history to happen — Christ's death and Resurrection to new life.

What Others Have Said About Prayer

Seven days without prayer makes one weak.
Allen Bartlett

* * *

If you are swept off your feet, it's time to get on
   your knees.
Fred Beck

* * *

Prayer, in its simplest definition, is merely a wish
   turned God-ward.
Phillip Brooks

* * *

If you would have God hear you when you pray,
   you must hear Him when He speaks.
Thomas Brooks

* * *

Prayer is conversation with God.
Clement of Alexandria

* * *

Pray and then start answering your prayer.
Deane Edwards

* * *

Prayer is like the turning on of an electric switch.
   It does not create the current; it simply provides
   a channel through which the electric current
   may flow.
Max Handel

* * *

Prayer does not change God, but changes him
   who prays.
Soren Kierkegaard

* * *

Prayer at its highest is a two-way conversation —
and for me the most important part is listening
to God's replies.
Frank Raubach

* * *

The fewer the words the better the prayer
Martin Luther

* * *

Prayer opens our eyes that we may see our selves
and others as God sees us.
Clara Palmer

* * *

Prayer is dangerous business. Results do come.
Christie Swain

* * *

Prayer is a rising up and drawing near to God in
mind, and in heart, and in spirit.
Alexander Whyte

* * *

Prayer surrounds the world.
Anon

When You Need Help

Dear Lord,
Take my hand and lead the way. *Amen*.

Dear Lord,
Help me to be strong. Give me courage to face the future and to accomplish your plan for my life. Let me see the pitfalls and other dangers so I can avoid them. Keep my soul free from sin, my mind clear of evil thoughts and my body free from temptation. In your holy name. *Amen*.

Lord,
Are you really out there? Please listen to me. I'm confused, worried. I don't know what or who to believe. Do you hear me, understand me and care for me? Please help me Lord. Thank you. *Amen*.

Father,
You and I have got a whole lifetime together. Sometimes I reckon even that won't be long enough for you to straighten me out. But other times I don't know if I could handle all those years. Will I make it? Or will I lose faith like so many others? How do I know if I'm treading the right path or if I'm going off by myself again?

Help me to keep my eyes fixed on you Lord. Don't let me be distracted by anything else. For I know if I hold on to you I can live by faith and everything will turn out fine in the end.

Father,
When I am lost and lose sight of you, when I forget my prayers and I'm swept away with life and all its difficulties, when I cannot answer my friends' questions about my faith even though I know the answer, when I'm too busy, and like homework I cannot do, you get shoved to the bottom of the pile. Remind me that all I have to do is to STOP!! For I know that you will find me and will meet me wherever I am.

Dear Lord,
My life is full of upsets. I often wonder if you are really listening. Please help me to be patient when I'm in a mess and listen to you. Please relieve me of any worries in my mind and help me to have faith in you and know you are always listening to our prayers.

Dear Lord,
I feel lonely and unloved by everyone. Help me to realise your love is everlasting and will never leave me. Help me also to feel your presence so that I can come through this hard time with your help. *Amen*.

Dear Lord,
When I need you, be by my side to guide me. Hold me in your tender hands and hide me from the blinding light. Keep me ever safe and warm near you, love me, save me, help me. Draw me to your kingdom Lord and keep me ever faithful. *Amen*.

Father,
So often we fail, not just in our own eyes, and those of others in this world, but most importantly in your eyes. Lord, help us to realise how much you really love us by giving us friends, families and the other wonders of your creation. Help us when we stray from your path and bring us back to your way of truth and love. *Amen.*

When You Want to Say Thanks

Dear Lord, Thank You. *Amen.*

Dear Lord,
With tears in my eyes
I look out upon your world.
I see all the pain,
the hurt and sadness.
I see joy and love too,
and this joy and love keeps me going.
For love is from you Father,
given to us by your Son
who died for our sins.
Thank you for saving us. *Amen.*

Thank you Lord for being there
to help and comfort me.
I know I can always trust you.
If I'm in trouble, there you'll be.
In every stage of living Lord
you're always there to guide.
I hope one day I meet you
when you call me to your side. *Amen.*

I thank you for everyone who has taken a part in
bringing me to your presence, for my parents who
brought me into the world and educated me in the ways
of life, for friends who constantly uplift me when I am

down or depressed, for leaders and fellow church people who provide much needed inspiration during times of trouble. However, help me to remember and in some way help, those who are less well off than me, those who lack a house, food or love from friends. In Jesus' name, *Amen*.

Lord God. Thank you for all your
blessings; for life and health,
for laughter and fun,
for all our powers of mind and body,
for our homes and the love of dear ones,
for everything that is beautiful, good and true.
Above all we thank you
for giving your Son to be our Saviour and Friend.
May we always find our true
happiness in obeying you,
for Jesus Christ's sake. *Amen*.

Dear God, The Bible tells us to be joyful. Help us to be glad you are in us and around us. You, Lord, are the fountain of love which never ceases. Thank you. Because of you we know that whenever we need a friend or guidance you will always be by our side. You are always ready to listen or to pick us up when we are down. So Lord, we thank you. *Amen*.

Thank you, Father, for all you've done for us. Thank you that your Son went through all the agony and pain of the cross to save us from our sins. Thank you that you care for us, as your children. Thank you that you love us, and know us. Help us, Lord, to get to know you better. Thank you that you have sent us your Holy Spirit to guide us. Please fill us with your Spirit, Lord. Thank you for everything. *Amen*.

Dear Lord God, I thank you that you are always with me when I need you, always willing to listen when I am talking and always speaking to me when I need talking to. *Amen.*

Lord,
Thank you for putting us in this world to serve and love you. *Amen.*

Dear Lord, Thank you for giving us this day,
our family and friends.
Help us to make the right decisions
for others and for ourselves.
Help us to be kind and good
and always have faith in you.
Give suffering people courage and strength,
to help them start anew.
Make us pure and forgive us our sins,
so that we may be like you! *Amen.*

Lord in this life of ours,
We take little time to stop
And say 'thank you'.

When You Feel Guilty

Lord, I know I've done things wrong.
I don't want to admit to it;
neither to my friends nor family or you.
Lord it's hard to live with myself.
I want to ask for your forgiveness
but I feel I don't deserve it.
To be honest I don't deserve it.
But thanks to you I know it's still there for the taking
so I ask that I may be given a fresh start
and be directed again on the right path.

Lord we confess that
when you call, we keep quiet.
When you beckon, we hesitate.
And when you repeat the call
we stubbornly stay silent.

We have sat content and unthinking
wrapped smug in ourselves.
We remain oblivious whilst others suffer
and are proud of our satisfaction.

Let us lay aside our petty arrogance
and take up the power of humility
So that we may learn
and come closer to you.

Lord, it's easy to laugh
So easy to hate.

It takes guts to be gentle and kind.
May we not be content with our frailty.

Let us not be blinded by
the trinkets of vanity
or intrigues of government
May we clearly see the path ahead.
the trail which was laid down by the one perfect sacrifice
along which we can follow your guidance
of justice and truth.

We confess our weakness
in not observing your example
When questioned let us have the strength
to pass on your message.
Help us to answer your call. *Amen.*

When we have sinned against you, Lord, or any one we
know, we feel guilty and ashamed at the wrongs we
have done. We know that you will always forgive us,
so please help us not to abuse your love. Guide us away
from sin and the consuming self-hatred and guilt which
ensue. *Amen.*

Dear Lord, Please cleanse me from my sins and forgive
me for my wrong-doings. I am truly sorry. *Amen.*

Dear Lord, When we have done wrong, the burden of
guilt is like a heavy bag of grain which rests on our

shoulders. You take this heavy load away dear Father when we ask for your forgiveness. Please help us not to do things which will cause a terrible pang of guilt. Help us to follow your path of love and truth. *Amen*.

Dear Lord, Please help us not to sin and lie or cheat. *Amen*.

When You Feel Lonely

Lord, friend to everyone,
You know when I feel lonely and discouraged. Please
help me to realise that I do not need to seek your presence, but that I am living in it daily and can never be
alone. For your name's sake.

Dear Lord,
Thanks for always being there when we need you. Help
those who don't know that you care for them and that
you are always there. For those people who stand in the
corner of the playground, who sit on their own in class,
who go home to an empty house, who have no one to
talk to and are LONELY, Lord help them. Help us to be
friendly, not unkind, to talk to them, not ignore them.
Amen.

Dear God,
When I feel lonely or depressed, help me to remember
that you are with me wherever I am. You always know
what I'm thinking and doing, so help me to feel your
presence all of the time. Help me realise that you love
ME as an individual despite everything, and that you
will never stop loving me. *Amen*.

O Father God, As you know
I haven't many friends.
Whenever I want some company

I only get dead-ends.
And so I come to you, dear friend
You never let me go.
I should have come to you first
But I just felt so alone.
So Father God, I ask you
to come and be my friend
and stay with me, O Father God
beyond a long life's end.

Lord, I'm lonely and I don't know who to turn to.
I ask you to be with me, and with all people who are
alone. To be alone is terrifying and everyone needs love.
Comfort us, Lord God, for Jesus' sake. *Amen.*

Dear God,
When we feel alone, when there is no one to talk to,
when our lives seem empty and we need a shoulder to
cry on, help us to remember you are always there, help
us to turn to you as our friend and father. *Amen.*

Dear Father,
When I am feeling lonely, please help me to find
friendship. When I feel neglected and out of place,
please help me to remember you are there. When I
feel a misfit, or visit an unfamiliar place, please remind
me O Lord that I will never be alone, you will always
be my friend. Please help me to draw in and welcome
those who are lonely and on their own. But most of all
help me to tell others they won't be lonely if they love
you. *Amen.*

If you are feeling really alone but there are people
around you, you probably need some support and

understanding. It's best to tell someone you know who will really sympathise and understand and try to help you. Possibly a best friend or maybe someone you don't know all that well. Then there is God, even if you are not aware he is there, you must have some idea, or you wouldn't be reading this. He can offer you support and comfort. Just by being relaxed and quiet by yourself you can gain inner peace, and that in itself will help.

I look up from my hurried task
and see no one there.
I stop and wonder where everyone is gone.
For me it is only a short while,
for countless others the feeling never stops.
It attacks day and night
cutting and bruising the fabric of the mind and body.
People are not made to be alone
and we have not the right to
subject anyone to that.
Pray God I will be given the strength
to befriend the lonely and give them comfort. *Amen*.

When You Feel Depressed

Thank you Lord that you're always there when I feel sad or let down, because I know that you will never let me down. When life seems unfair I can always depend on you for your guidance and support to help me through difficult situations. *Amen*.

Dear Heavenly Father,
Why do so many people seem against me? Every way I turn it seems as though there is another figure to insult and hurt me. So often I fight back with fierce words which seem to come from the centre of my depression. Oh Lord, please help me to control myself in these situations and find the love from the centre of my heart to give them. Lord I always know that no matter how people turn against me, I will always have you as a friend. *Amen*.

Dear Lord,
There are times in our lives when we feel lonely and depressed. Help to guide us through these dark times in our lives. When we are depressed remind us of that special love you have for all of us. You love us so much that you died for us.
Help us to remember this and to know that you will always be with us whatever happens in our lives. *Amen*.

Lord, Difficult situations appear every day that question our faith. To be unhappy is the worst situation I have ever faced. We love you with all our heart, how do we show our love when we are depressed? I am your sheep and I'm lost. Find me Lord. *Amen.*

Dear Lord,
When I feel depressed and think that nobody cares about me, help me to realise that there are many people around me who can help and who love me just like you do. Help me to turn to them and to you, when times are rough. You taught people to love each other. Help me to remember this when I feel depressed and out on my own. Through your name I ask it. *Amen.*

Lord, I am sad.
I am crying.
Like dew on a web: help me find beauty in my tears; beauty in my life.
Let me cry for ever.

Dear Lord, Help me to overcome depression. After all, when I think of the insignificance of my depression compared with the starving, abused and lonely I feel privileged. Please lift my thoughts and spirit up so I can do your work. *Amen.*

When You Want to Say Sorry

Lord,
Help me to know when I am wrong and give me the strength and courage to say that I am sorry — three words that so often we find hard to say but can make such a difference to both our lives and to those we love. Help me to realise that our life on earth is far too short to argue with those we love and care for and that we should all have the compassion for others that you have for us. Forgive me Lord for all my wrongdoings and help me to be a better person. *Amen*.

Dear God,
I'm sorry for all the times I do the things that I know you wouldn't want me to do. When I think or say something to hurt someone; when I fail you and fall short of your expectations. Help us to be more like your son, Jesus, every day. *Amen*.

Oh Lord,
It is so difficult to say sorry to anyone and even more so to say sorry to you. It is impossible to find the words to express exactly what we feel but I pray that you will read our hearts rather than our words and hence discover our true sentiments so that you may know how sorry we are, Lord, for everything sinful in our lives. *Amen*.

Dear Lord,
There are many things that we need to say sorry for. Maybe we have been selfish or hurtful, or misunderstood friends and family. Sometimes we say things on the spur of the moment which we regret later. Help us to be more controlled about what we say. Sorry is such a difficult word to say, so help us to say it openly and meaningfully. *Amen*.

Bad luck Lord, it's me again! Guess what I've done this time. — You know. Oh well then I had better just say I'm 'sorry'. *Amen*.

Dear Heavenly Father,
You know all of us.
You love all of us.
And care for each of us.
I do not know you well
and sometimes I forget you are here.
I am sorry for when I've forgotten you.
Help me to remember you are here all
the time, not just Sundays. *Amen*.

God,
I made a real mess again, didn't I. I never intended to hurt anyone. I just didn't think. I ended up hurting the people I love the most, including you. But I think it was me who hurt the most in the end. Sorry. *Amen*.

Dear Lord,
I know you don't want a great big long explanation as to why I committed a sin *yet again* — you know all that but what I really want to say is . . . . Please forgive me. *Amen*.

32

When You Want to Celebrate

God,
Let's celebrate!
Let's celebrate your love for us all, no matter who we are.
Let's celebrate our life on earth.
Let's celebrate our love for you.
Let's celebrate your giving to us your one and only son.
Let's celebrate love — our love for you and your love for us.
Without this love, what can we celebrate?
Lord, in Your name. *Amen*.

Dear Lord,
At this present time I feel so close to you. I can feel you in my life. At these times I want to celebrate, for your love is so strong. When I try to think of all the wonders you have performed my whole existence seems so trivial and when I think of all my sin I am so ashamed. But, Lord, you still love me and I am grateful for that. I am so glad that I have opened my heart for you. Without you there would be no point for me to living. I want to tell everyone of your love so they can feel the warmth and security that I can feel at this time. Thank you Lord and help me to remember that you are always there with me. *Amen*.

Dear Lord,
We thank you for the power and love you give to us.

May we recognise how much you help us in everything we do and may we be content with all that we have and not always ask for more, as you give us all that we need. *Amen*.

Dear Lord,

We celebrate all the things you have given to us. The sun, stars, trees and flowers. Also for all the people you have placed here on earth. Teach us to love them all and not just those we consider our friends. Please help us through our hard times and keep us safe in your love and security forever. *Amen*.

When Your Life is Really Difficult

Dear Lord,
I am finding life hard and frustrating; nothing seems to work out right. I pray that your love and strength will sustain me through this time and that your spirit will guide me so that I become aware of your will and fulfil it to the best of my ability. *Amen.*

Dear Lord,
We cannot possibly understand you fully, or comprehend the ways in which you work. When we are depressed, help us always to remember that you want what is best for us. Sometimes, the things we worry over turn out to be your way of bringing us closer to you. However sad or worried we are, and however far we drift away from you, your constant love is always there to aid us and bring us back into your presence. *Amen.*

Dear Lord,
Please help us to know that whatever problems we may have, we can always rely on you to help us. May we confide everything to you with open hearts and trust you to show us your unfailing love in our times of need. *Amen.*

Father,
My life is turning out a mess. Sometimes I wish I could

just fall asleep and never wake up. But that would be a waste because, Lord, you have given us one life. Lord, help me to steer my life into a happy one. *Amen*.

Lord,
Times are difficult. I need you Lord. I need to know that you are near, that you are watching over me and most of all, Lord, that you love me. Please guide me in everything that I say and do. Thank you. *Amen*.

Lord,
Thank you that you are always with me, especially when I am going through difficulty. I thank you, Lord, that you experienced the difficulties of life when you came to live on earth, and experienced suffering when separated from Your Father. I pray, Lord, therefore that you will guide me and lead me always, especially now. *Amen*.

Remove us, oh Lord, from the cynicism and hypocrisy of our secular preoccupations; and give us true faith which consists of sincerity in our love for all that is good, and for all that you have done for us. Just as your Son rose from the grave, give us the courage to rise from all the pride and pretence which so loosely clothes our sometimes empty souls. Help us to expose your true light, through our faith. *Amen*.

O Lord,
You have searched me and you know me.
You know when I sit and when I rise;
You perceive my thoughts from afar.
You discern my going out and my lying down;
You are familiar with all my ways.
Before a word is on my tongue

You know it completely, O Lord.
You hem me in — behind and before;
You have laid your hand upon me.
Such knowledge is too wonderful for me,
Too lofty for me to attain.
Where can I go from your Spirit?
Where can I flee from your presence?
If I go up to the heavens, you are there;
If I make my bed in the depths, you are there.
If I rise on the wings of the dawn,
If I settle on the far side of the sea,
Even there your hand will guide me,
Your right hand will hold me fast.
How precious to me are your thoughts O God!
How vast is the sum of them!
Were I to count them, they would
outnumber the grains of sand.
When I awake
I am still with you.
Search me, O God, and know my heart;
Test me and know my anxious thoughts.
See if there is any offensive way in me,
And lead me in the way everlasting. *Amen*.

(Sorry, Nick, I couldn't think of anything to write, so I
nicked this from Psalm 139! Sorry! This is what I always
read, when I feel low.)

When You Are Doing Exams

I pray that in the coming exams you will keep me calm and bring back to my mind all that I have learnt.

Dear Lord,
Help me when I feel panicky about my exams. Help me to realise that it only matters if the mark is good for me, not for anybody else. Do not let our parents get us down, saying we must get at least 99% in every subject in exchange for a new bike. Wish me luck. *Amen*.

Dear Lord,
When I take exams let me go the extra mile with revision.
I know that if I fail you will be there to say I haven't.
When I'm feeling down about exams, help cheer me up.
Thank you Lord, *Amen*.

Dear God,
I have just had my exams, which I didn't enjoy, but you got me through them. You gave me the strength I needed and now I want to celebrate because I actually passed. I feel as if it were all worth it after all. Thank you for your strength. *Amen*.

Lord,
My heart is pulsating and
My tummy is quivering and

my mind is whirring.
— Oh please! refresh me with your peace.
I pray, dear God, that as my exams approach,
I may feel calm,
Let your peace shine through me,
that others may glimpse the serenity within me,
and want to discover its source.
Please remove that ominous, depressive cloud
which seems to hover over exams, and replace it with
sunshine.
Let me look forward to my exams,
seeing them as a time when I can share my knowledge
of things with a, probably, weary examiner.
Please help me not to worry, Lord,
for worrying solves no problems
If my marks are good,
please help me not to rest on my laurels.
If my marks are bad,
please help me not to despair.
You love me, Lord, and I love you.
That is more important than any exam result.
Thank you for hearing me. *Amen*.

Dear God,
Help us through this difficult time of exams. Help us
to do as well as we can so that we can obtain the
qualifications we need to do what you have in mind
for us. We know that even if we do not do as well as
we expected you still love us and still have a purpose for
us. Perhaps you are teaching us patience by getting us
to retake them or perhaps you have something entirely
different in mind. If we do as well or better than we
expected then we must remember that without you we
would have got nowhere, whether we acknowledge it
or not because without your gifts of life, intelligence, a
conscience, and, of course, a soul, we are nothing. We
pray that you may relieve the exam stress that affects so

many people so that we can do our best. Thank you O God. *Amen.*

Dear God,
Please help me through my exams. Stop me from cheating which wouldn't be right. I am hopeless at the moment, but would be more assured if I can send this prayer. *Amen.*

Father,
I thank you that you are always with me, especially when I am in difficulty. Guide and help me through these exams so that I may do justice to all I have learned, Lord. I dedicate them to you and pray that I do them for your glory and not my own. I pray for everyone doing exams and that you may guide and help all of them. Help us to keep their importance in perspective Lord and to use them to draw closer to you. Thank you. *Amen.*

Dear God,
Please help me in my exams. Help me to understand the questions. *Amen.*

When You Are Worried About Others

Lord,
Some people really suffer because of something physically wrong with them and others suffer just as badly because of some mental disability. Please Lord, we know that with you we can help these people to fight their disability or illness. Strengthen us so that when we know someone who has something wrong with them we may have the faith to help them in whatever way you show us. *Amen*.

Lord,
We think of young people all round the world especially those who don't know you, who don't have the opportunities to grow in your love. Help us, Lord, to share with others the knowledge of your presence in our lives. There is still so much about you we have yet to discover, give us the courage, Lord, to know you more and to show our faith in our everyday lives. *Amen*.

Father,
I thank you for my friends. Without them I wouldn't be as strong, but Lord please teach me how to love without intruding, how to be gentle but sincere, to cope when all seems to fall apart. When someone I love is hurting I feel pain, also when someone is upset I long to help them. Lord, give me strength to be there when someone needs me. Help me to help them through their troubles.

Speak through me so that I can be sure that what I say is of use. Help me to care rather than to worry for I know it's the caring and understanding that I need to give. Thank you for listening to my feelings Father. I know I can help the ones I need to with your strength and love. *Amen*.

Father,
There are times when I act by instinct and not by thought. But there are other times when I act on purpose to hurt. I am sorry for those times, help me to think and help rather than hurt those who are my friends.

As tears course down people's faces
Their pain is like a fire inside.
The fire will always be there,
It can only be cooled by the
love of dear friends.
The pain will always cause anger and grief.
The only cure is love and patience. *Amen*.

Heavenly Father,
I am praying for people who are ill or sick. For people who do not have any money to buy food for their families. Those who do not have any family to turn to and who live on their own and have no one who cares about them.
 I also pray for those who are depressed or unhappy at this moment.
For the children who have no mums or dads because they have died.
Please help them through this. *Amen*.

Loving Father,
We pray for people living on their own, who cannot get out and about. Please help them not to lose faith but get to know you more. Please help people not to be lonely, especially old people, or people who have been bereaved. Make them see that they can always find a friend in you, whatever the time, wherever the place. We ask this, in your name. *Amen.*

Lord,
Help us when we are worried about others. Help us to comfort them. Help us to pray for them. And Lord help those who have any kind of illness. *Amen.*

When Someone Lets You Down

Dear Lord,
Why isn't everyone in the world like you. *Amen.*

Lord,
Only you know how much I am hurting inside and how unwilling I am to forgive. Help me to remember the sacrifice that you made for me by dying on the cross and to see that in comparison my sacrifice is small. Lord, help me to forgive those who have hurt me. *Amen.*

Dear Lord,
As I speak to you now I feel hurt and neglected. Please help me, Lord, to understand why I was let down and please help me to forgive them as you forgave me. And please fill me and them with your everlasting love. I ask this in your name. *Amen.*

Dear God,
When we are let down don't allow us to become bitter. Instead of turning away from someone help us to see their reasons for doing what they did. You're the only one we can completely depend on. But don't let us dismiss others because of the human faults we all possess. *Amen.*

Dear God,
Please help. My friends have let me down badly. They have suddenly turned against me because of where I live. They call me names and tell me I don't belong. Please help me to overcome the hurt I feel. Thanks. *Amen*.

Dear Lord,
When someone lets us down it seems so hard to be able to forgive them. Please help us to be able to forgive and forget and to say sorry when we let others down. *Amen*.

Dear Father,
Please help me forgive those who let down, use, or disappoint me: for you have often forgiven me for far worse things. Help me also to want to forgive them and to do it willingly without malice. Remind me in times of anger to remember that revenge does not do any good and help me to forgive and forget as our Lord Jesus Christ always did. *Amen*.

Dear Lord,
When someone lets me down don't let me get annoyed; let me listen to their reason and be sympathetic. If they have an awful excuse don't let me question it for Lord if they lie they are only deceiving themselves. Let them see this. Thank you dear Lord. *Amen*.

Dear God,
When we are let down by a friend or relative, help us to be strong and help us to understand why we have been let down. If we are upset, help us not to forget that you are with us in whatever situation arises, and that you are there to assist us. Help us to remember that there may be

more than just ourselves involved. Perhaps the culprit feels guilty, or maybe he/she has let down more than one person. Help us not to be too self-centred. *Amen.*

Lord,
I've been let down
again. By one of my friends
again. He forgot to turn up
again. He was too busy
again. Didn't have time.
Lord I'm getting fed up
with excuses. I can't see what is so difficult about coming round to help me. If I ask you to help me you are there — so why is it so difficult for us to help each other? Lord, I pray that I may be tolerant of my friends' shortcomings. Help me not to forget that I have just as many faults as anyone else. Teach us to be humble Lord, and always to remember we are all equal in your love. *Amen.*

When You Have Doubts

Dear God,
We all find things hard to believe, and our minds are filled with doubts. Is there really a God? Did everything in the Bible really happen? Why do we believe in something we cannot see? God, you know that we do have faith, but the world's temptations often steer us away. Guide us away from those temptations. Fill us with your Holy Spirit to help us to answer our doubts and strengthen our faith and love for you and each other. *Amen*.

Dear Lord,
It is so easy to doubt you,
there are so many questions we want to ask.
Help us trust in you so that in time we will find
out the answers.
In times of worry and trouble,
when we need your love the most,
help us to feel your presence
so you can guide us in the right direction,
towards a brighter, happier and loving future. *Amen*.

Dear Lord,
Life is full of ups and downs and often I am filled with doubts. Help me to trust in you and to have a steady faith, to be child-like — not always questioning but obeying. Guide me through depressions and teach us to stand up against the forces of evil and corruption, for

I know that nothing can separate me from your infinite love. In Jesus' name. *Amen*.

God doesn't want you to have anything.
He's not waiting for you to attain some goal.
He's not comparing you with anyone else.
You need to love him, to believe in him,
to do what he wants.
You need to see him as God.
You may falter, fail and fall.
Everyone else seems to be going along fine.
Why me Lord? Why am I the only failure?
Yet when He looks at you, he sees . . .
No, not the tangled mess, but gold.
For your desire to know him better
Is more precious than any achievement.
Ask for that desire to increase
for that is your God's delight.

Dear God,
Just about everyone has doubts but often living away from home, especially for the first time, can be an incredibly testing period. You find yourself surrounded by strangers many of whom are not Christian, and, because you so desperately want to fit in, you may find your values begin to slip.

As Jesus suffered in the wilderness help us through these times. Let us remember that there are always going to be others in the same situation who need our help. And let us remember that our Christian roots are only a phone call or a letter away. But most importantly you will never desert us. *Amen*.

Dear God,
In times of doubt and hesitation please act as our guide.

When we are in darkness, then shine like a lamp to light the right path. Help and advise us when the answer to a problem seems unclear, for we would all be lost without you and existence would be in chaos if doubt were to gain the upper hand. *Amen*.

Dear God,
I know that I have my doubts about you, that I am unsure when it comes to making a decision at a fork in the pathway of life. Often I am tempted to take the easy route, almost always the route away from you. Help me to grow in your faith that I may make the right decisions and put your will before mine, to do your work in the world, for your glory.
In Jesus' name. *Amen*.

When You Don't Get on
With Parents

Lord,
Help me to restrain my anger and frustration when I
have been arguing with my parents. I know they mean
well, but they don't express their feeling of love and
caring in the way I'd like. Help me to understand that
they mean well and help me to go back and say I'm
sorry. In Jesus' name. *Amen.*

Dear Lord,
There are times in my life when I feel everyone is against
me, especially my parents. They seem to be so nasty and
are always criticising my actions. I know they are only
trying to show me the right way to live but it's very
frustrating being ordered about. Help me to honour
and respect my parents, to give back a little of the love
they show for me, to obey and not to question. For it
is in giving that we receive and in pardoning that we
are pardoned.
I pray these things in Jesus' name. *Amen.*

Dear God,
Please help me to make amends with my parents. They
make it difficult for me and I cannot help disagreeing
with them. Please help me to see things from their point
of view. Thank you. *Amen.*

Dear God,
Please let my parents realise how much I love them and
do so want to get on with them. I know I have been bad
but they just don't understand my feelings. *Amen*.

Dear Lord, Our Father
Please have pity on me and my family,
for we fight with wrong in our minds and not right.
We fight without concern for other people and later we
regret it.
Give us wisdom, faith and trust in our family. *Amen*.

Lord,
Help us to get on with our parents at all times. When in
time of stress let us be able to comfort each other. Help
us to understand what they are feeling when we annoy
them. Let us be loving and cherishing, able to respect
and be grateful to them at all times. Help us to obey them
and not to answer back when told to do something we
don't like.
In your name. *Amen*.

O Father,
Why is it when at our age if you hit your brother or have
an argument, your mother shouts at you and you don't
get a word in edgeways. When this happens I don't want
to take the law into my own hands.
Please help me. *Amen*.

When You Are Afraid of the Future

Dear Lord,
When we are worried and afraid of the future, not knowing where we are going to go, or what we are going to do, please guide us along the right path and reassure us that you will look after us, whatever happens in the dangerous road of life.
Help us to keep faith in you, and know that we always have a place in your heart. *Amen*.

Dear God,
At this moment in time the future seems frightening but I know you have a plan for each and every one of us. Lord, help us not to be afraid of the future and give us faith to trust in you Father. I love you. *Amen*.

Dear Lord,
When we are afraid of the future strengthen our hearts and minds, and give us courage to face up to whatever lies ahead. Let us remember that you will always be there with us shining your light before us. *Amen*.

Lord,
You have shown us a way
for us to live from day to day.
But 'money talks';
'on yer bike!' (and all the rest)
is what they say

and think is best.
Even though, Lord, you might
not like our ways of greed and plunder
or even wonder
why we always have to fight.
So show us, Lord, your way of life
in this absurd and crazy world
with love in our hearts
and peace among us. *Amen*.

Lord,
Please help me when I am afraid of the future
to be guided by your word
to walk ahead with confidence into the darkness.
Give me courage to carry on
and strength to take step after step
until I emerge on the other side
with a greater love of you. *Amen*.

Lord,
Help us to put our faith in you, and let us trust you to
take care of our future. Whatever the situation let us look
to the future hopefully, knowing that you will always be
there to help us in times of trouble. *Amen*.

When You Have Got an Important Decision to Make

Eeny meany miney mo,
Help me find the way to go. *Amen*.

Father,
You know that I am afraid, and I don't know which way
to turn. Please Lord, come down and comfort me, and
help me make the right decisions. Please Lord, help all
those who are going through the same experience as I
am. Give them strength through your Holy Spirit. Lord,
I ask this in your name. *Amen*.

Please Lord,
This decision could be a turning point in my life. Shine
your light to show me the right path to take. I know that
you will show me the way. I know that you will always
be with me, loving me, and I trust you to show me the
right path. *Amen*.

Lord,
When we have a difficult or important decision to make,
please help us to make the best and wisest choice. If the
decision is going to hurt others, let us forget about it, or
if it is for the good of others, let us stick to our decision,
through to the end. *Amen*.

Lord God,
We are making decisions every day. Important decisions can often tell you where your life is going to lead. Help us to make the right decisions Lord, so that we may follow you in the ways of your Son. *Amen.*

O Lord, I pray that you will be with me to help and guide me whenever I have to make an important decision in my life. I know that I can trust you to be by my side to give me the strength and help that I will so often need.

I also ask Lord that you will help me to be grateful and cheerful for all the wonderful things in life that you have given to us, but we so often take for granted. Help me to remember that you are always there when I need help and that you know which road is the right road for me to take. Lord hear my prayer and always be by my side. *Amen.*

When You Are Grateful For Your Friends

Lord,
Thank you for my friends. Thank you that they are always there when I am in trouble and need help, or when I need a shoulder to cry on. Help me to be loyal to my friends and to give them as much love and support as they give me, not only in times of need, but also when life seems to present no problems. For your name's sake. *Amen.*

Lord I thank you for my friends.
When I am confused
they give me wisdom.
When I feel sad
they help me smile.
When I feel worthless
they share their love.
Lord above all this,
I thank you that you are my
friend forever. *Amen.*

Dear Father,
I thank you for all the friends you have blessed me with. I am grateful for their witness of you, their support, and love in times of suffering and despair, and for their presence to share in times of joy. *Amen.*

Friends are to be trusted,
friends try to be kind.
I thank you Lord for friends.

Friends are to be treated nicely
and not to be hurt or insulted.
I thank you Lord for friends.

Friends are more important
than personal belongings.
Friends are worth more than money.
I thank you Lord for friends. *Amen*.

Dear Lord,
When we are spiteful and nasty to our friends,
help us to tell them how sorry we are,
for where would we be
without friends? We would be lonely and unhappy.
Jesus had lots of friends, even the outcasts. As you
will always be our friend, let us love you as we love
ourselves.
And let us be happy. *Amen*.

Thank you God for friends. Friends who stand by you
in your time of trouble, who guide you through difficult
decisions. Friends who tell you things that you should
not do, and tell you when they don't like the things you
are doing.
   Lord, help us to accept our friends as they are, with
all their faults. Help us Lord to forgive our friends who
have wronged us or hated us. Help us to share the gifts
and things we have with others, as well as our problems,
as friends can prove very helpful and understanding. O
Lord, help us not to be jealous of others and the friendships that they have. Make us grateful for what we have;
help us appreciate this and be content with it. *Amen*.

Dear Lord,
We thank you for the friends we have and all the love and joy we share. May we learn how to be the best friends possible, and never expect too much from others.

Thank you for being our greatest friend, Lord. *Amen.*

When Others Suffer For Their Faith

Lord,
Thank you that we live in a country where we have the right to speak our mind and worship you our King without any restrictions. Teach us to remember all prisoners who suffer for their beliefs. And especially let us remember people who suffer in South Africa because of their colour or race. Let us remember all who suffer in Communist countries for their beliefs. We thank you Lord that we can worship you without being persecuted for it.
Lord, don't let us forget Christians in other countries. *Amen.*

'If you encounter evil and refuse to oppose it, you surrender your humanity.
If you encounter evil and oppose it, you enter into humanity.
If you encounter evil and oppose it with the weapons of God, you enter into divinity'.
Father, fill your people with the strength of your love, so that through times of suffering their faith may prove strong enough to act as a shield against the burning arrows of persecution.

Dear Jesus,
Sometimes I take for granted the easy life I lead as a Christian. Although at times I may find it difficult to

cope with situations that occur, and I question my faith, I know that in other countries people are suffering brutally for living their lives according to their faith. Help me not to be afraid to show everyone that I believe in you, and help others who are not afraid to do this, but suffer for it. *Amen.*

Dear God,
You have given me the chance to meet with other Christians of my own age. When I see your light and feel your warmth in these people, I am strengthened. But this does not occur all over the world and not always throughout this country. Help me to remember those who are persecuted either physically or emotionally for their faith. Strengthen those living under repressive governments, and those who are ridiculed either by friends or in the home. Never let us forget these people. It may happen that we will find ourselves in a similar situation one day. And if we should, never let me deny that you died for us. *Amen.*

Dear Lord,
I know that the persecution that I am experiencing is hardly anything compared with what Jesus and some other people in the world have had to put up with, but still it is hard to confess my faith in front of non-believers. Please Lord give me the strength that I need to be a true witness for you. *Amen.*

When Animals Suffer

Thank you for all your creatures. Animals are a wonderful part of your creation, and so please let us appreciate them, and love them as you do. Let us not abuse them or make them suffer for our benefit. Cruelty is a major event in people's lives. So please help us to prevent cruelty in our world because everyone has a right to live, including the animals that you have made. *Amen.*

Dear Father God,
You gave each animal a name and gave it life like us. They are so like us yet not so, as you gave them no voice that we can understand and no knowledge that they can understand *us*. For this reason we should communicate with them through love and affection, and respect their lives here on earth as our own.

We need help, as we too often take for granted our power over animals. Help us not to abuse this power but to care for the creatures you have given us — after all they were created by you. *Amen.*

Dear Lord,
Please help the animals who suffer whether through bodily harm or through lack of care. Please help the people who kill animals for fun or for their fur to understand what they are doing. Thank you for all the charities who help to make animals' lives better. *Amen.*

Dear Lord,
This is a prayer for those who cannot speak to save themselves from being destroyed. This is for the animals of
our world who suffer because of humans whose only
aim, it seems, is to expand and in doing so destroy the
beautiful environment and animals you created for us.
So help us to realise what we are doing or what we
have already done. Help those who go purposefully
out of their way to kill animals. Help us also to find
other means of doing experiments without the use of
innocent animals.

Lord, help us to think more clearly and carefully about
what we are doing to the creatures of this world and our
environment for the sake of those who cannot speak for
themselves. *Amen.*

When the Environment is Neglected and Destroyed

Father, we belong to you,
you made us,
you gave us life,
you love us.
Father, this is your world
you made it,
you gave it life,
you care for it;
yet we are destroying it.
We pull down the homes of the animals you created,
we burn the trees that you sent the sun and rain to
nourish.
Forgive us Father,
show us how to make your world
flourish,
not die. *Amen*.

Look at your beautiful earth Lord, look at what we are
doing to it. An earth that you created especially for your
children, a paradise for our time on earth and yet we
neglect and destroy it.

Lord help us to be thankful for what you have given
us — to respect our surroundings and to do our utmost
to preserve it. For in guarding what you give us Lord,
we are praising you for it. *Amen*.

Dear Lord,
You created the environment for us to live in, the green trees and grass, the blue sky and the sparkling sea. You created it to provide homes and happiness, yet we destroy the trees, we build factories where fields should be, we pollute the air with fumes, and we dump our rubbish in the sea. Why Lord do we do this? Please help us to treat the environment with care and respect, so that we can all live in a cleaner, healthier place. *Amen*.

Lord,
When we neglect and destroy our environment we also destroy your creation. Help us to look after our world, care for all that is in it and to show you that we are proud to be your children and live in your world.
Through Jesus Christ our Lord. *Amen*.

Dear Lord,
Please help us to tidy up our town (village, city)
and countryside,
and make it look more respectable.
Help us to plant flowers
and tidy up existing flower beds.
Help us not to drop litter
but to put it in bins where it belongs.
Help us to do all these things and more. *Amen*.

God,
You gave us this world to look after.
You put your trust in our hands.
You let us take care of your creation.
You gave us animals of all colours, breeds, shapes and sizes.
You gave us beauty in our own surroundings.
You gave us colour and the blooming flowers of spring.

You gave us a heaven on earth,
but we have to ask for your forgiveness.
We have taken your trust for granted.
No longer do all the animals roam the earth free and in the right surroundings.
We kill them for the colour of their fur, or for their elaborate feathers.
We kill them for money and selfish greed and destroy their surroundings.
We erect miles of concrete and destroy trees and plants which stand in our way.
We build for ourselves and destroy other living things for our comfort.
Not only do we destroy the wildlife, but we destroy each other.
We let each other starve, live in poverty, we kill each other, we steal from each other — but what for — greed and money.
God we have turned the planet earth into a bomb of another kind;
not a bomb owned by the government, but a bomb every person owns.
The time for that bomb going off is getting near.
God, guide us and forgive us — please. *Amen.*

Advent

Dear Lord,
Thank you for this time of Advent. As we enjoy the preparation for Christmas, the fun and laughter, may we remember the true meaning of this time in the Church's year. Help us to let the light of your Son into our lives today. For your name's sake. *Amen.*

Dear God,
As we begin our preparations for Christmas, help us to remember what Christmas is really about. As we light our advent candles, or our christingles, help us think about Jesus as the light of the world.
Without him there would be no Christmas.
Make us strong as we go through Advent and help us to think about Jesus, the Son of God, at his birth. *Amen.*

Dear God,
During Advent we think about the coming of Christ. We pray to you to help us to keep our thoughts on the real meaning of Advent and to look forward to when Christ comes at Christmas. *Amen.*

Dear Lord,
In this time of Advent, help us to prepare ourselves for Christmas. Help us to be guided by you as Christmas arrives, and in the hustle and bustle of preparation let us sit down quietly for a while to think about the real

meaning of Christmas and Advent. Advent is not only a preparation for Christmas, but a time to remember Christ's promise that he would return 'like a thief in the night'. We must be ready for him always as we do not know the time or the place when he will come again. *Amen*.

Come, oh come Lord,
Lighten our darkness
With your word.
Strengthen our weakness,
Inspire us to praise and love you
And bring us your understanding. *Amen*.

Dear Lord,
During this Advent time help us to prepare ourselves not only to receive you as a small child in Bethlehem, but also as a great judge who will one day return to judge us all. Lord, we cannot say for sure when you will return. We can only ask that you help us to prepare ourselves to meet you.
For your name's sake. *Amen*.

Dear Lord,
Help us to prepare for the coming of Jesus. Lighten our hearts with his Spirit and let him come to us and grow with us like a new born baby. This is a happy time at which I am proud to be part of the church. Thank you for guiding me towards this happiness and leading me to Jesus at this time. *Amen*.

Christmas

It's Christmastime.
The holly is abundant.
The presents are under the tree.
The turkey is in the oven.
The grandparents are in the spare room.
But what of the meaning of Christmas?
'Yes, you know Jesus'. 'Jesus who?'
Father, let us not get carried away by the trappings of Christmas.
Let us remember the birth of your son, our Saviour.
The traditions of Christmas may be fun, but let us not forget the meaning of Christmas.
In Jesus' name. *Amen*.

Dear God,
At this special Christmastime help us to remember the truth behind the festival. We praise and thank you for sending your son to us. As he came in humility, may we remember those less fortunate and more humble than ourselves. *Amen*.

Lord,
Bless everyone this Christmas who won't be having a good time. People who are ill or in hospital. People who are on their own with no family. Fill their hearts with happiness so they can share in the true meaning of Christmas. In the name of Jesus. *Amen*.

Dear Father,
As we prepare for a time of giving and goodwill, help us to remember that Christmas is not just lights, presents and a stocking. There is a deep and wonderful meaning: a celebration of the birth of a little child whose words would far exceed the power of any leader and whose teaching is passed from generation to generation. This surely is the true meaning of Christmas. *Amen*.

Peace, perfect peace?
A pretty strange idea Lord. No matter how many people strive for peace their work is soon undone by the weakness of man. But what sort of peace? World peace? Peace with yourself? Peace with God? Lord, help us to work for peace. To reconcile nations, races, cultures, creeds and neighbours that all men may see eye to eye and call each other 'brother'; that we all may find peace in our hearts and peace with you.
Peace on earth. *Amen*.

New Year

Heavenly Father,
Through your Son a light has shone upon the world, a new hope has touched the hearts of many. As we start a new year be with us in all that we think, say and do. Help us to act upon what we believe and not lose sight of your wonderous love for us.
Through Jesus Christ our Lord. *Amen*.

Dear Father,
I pray that as a New Year approaches you will strengthen my faith and commitment to you. I pray that you will help me to be more compassionate patient and tolerant towards others. I pray that you will guide me in all that I do and help me especially as I try to spread your word, in the most tactful way, to others who may be unsure about their belief in you. I ask this in Jesus' name. *Amen*.

Dear God,
Let the New Year be a new starting point. A point to forgive and forget the things people have done against us and a time to look back and learn from our past mistakes. Let us also look forward to the future and help us to aim for the right things, and give us a purpose to live for.

Father,
We thank you for helping us in times of difficulty over the past year and for being with us. Help us to go forth

into the New Year knowing that our faith will deepen and our love for you will grow stronger. Be with us when we are having fun and when we are unhappy. Now and forever. *Amen*.

We thank you for this opportunity to begin again — for a fresh start, so that we can forget what has been bad and remember the good; so we may lead a new life, with you to help us on our way. We ask you to guide us, taking each day as it comes. *Amen*.

Father as I throw off the old year and with it all its sins, tears and confrontations, help me to go forward; forgiven, cleansed, refreshed, to make a new start full of confidence to do what I know to be right, to fight for justice, to take up life's challenge and to win. *Amen*.

Dear God,
Thank you for all the good things that have happened, like the help countries have given to the needy and the efforts to make the world more at peace. Help and strengthen these efforts. Please comfort all the people who were involved in the tragedies and violence of the past year and guide them through the New Year. *Amen*.

Dear Lord,
As we come into a New Year may we pray that it is a successful one for all of us whether we are at college, university, school or in work. We pray for all teenagers worldwide and that you will guide us with your hand through any decisions we have to make concerning our future. *Amen*.

Lent

Dear God and Father,
As we start this spiritual pilgrimage of Lent, help us to resist the temptations of the devil and to persevere through the wilderness of this world. Help us to appreciate how lucky we are as we embark on seven weeks of self-denial and to use your faithful Son Jesus as an example and guide.

Help us to think about why we give up things and make sacrifices and let this period be a time for reflection so that we may be open to the true meaning of your death upon the cross, for us, and the resurrection to new life on Easter Sunday. *Amen*.

Dear God,
Help us in this time leading up to Easter to remember why we celebrate Easter, not for the commercial reason, but for you. You gave away your life for us and for this we are grateful. *Amen*.

Father,
At this time, where by tradition we 'give up' something, let us begin something new that will aid others. *Amen*.

Dear Father God,
When we go out into the wilderness as Jesus did, on our own in this huge world, keep us free from temptations and sins. It is so easy for our minds to be distracted so

we fall into the wrong path. At Lent especially give us strength to persevere, and to give something up, not because we have to but because we love you. *Amen.*

Dear Lord,
Make this time of self-denial, when we give up something that is going to help us deepen our life with God and grow closer to him, a meaningful experience. *Amen.*

Dear Lord,
Easter is coming soon when we remember the death and resurrection of Christ. In the days leading up to Easter, we think about the agony Jesus went through knowing he would die. So as we give up various things for Lent we look forward to the day when Jesus rose again. We ask you now and for always to look after us like you did your son. *Amen.*

Dear God,
At this time of self-denial, let us remember the words of your son Jesus Christ. 'Do not sleep, get up and pray that you will not fall into temptation'. Give us the strength to perform the tasks you set for us and give us the courage to stand up for your love. For the sake of Jesus. *Amen.*

Easter

Dear Lord,
Thank you for Easter Sunday. The sorrow and the sadness of Lent and Good Friday is gone and is replaced by the happiness and rejoicing of Easter.

Now to some the true meaning of Easter is in the background, replaced by chocolate eggs, and the coming of spring.

But I try to remember Jesus and what happened on Easter Sunday, and love you for it. *Amen.*

Dear Lord and Father,
We praise you for sending your son to us in human form to die for our sins. We pray that from Christ Jesus' death on the cross we may learn to open our hearts to you and place you first in our lives so that we may have eternal life. Thank you Lord. *Amen.*

Dear God,
Thank you for sending your son to us, to teach us about love and the Holy Spirit. He died for us on the cross; for this we are grateful. Help us to remember this brave act of love. *Amen.*

Lord,
At this time we thank you for your son Jesus Christ, who died for our sins and we thank you that he has risen again. *Amen.*

Father,
Thank you for all you have done and all you have given us. We thank you that at this time your son died to save us and conquered death. We can now be reconciled to you and live with you in your glory because of the ultimate sacrifice your Son made for us. We thank you father and Lord. *Amen.*

Dear Lord,
When you gave us Jesus you must have known what we'd do. .
When we tortured him and wanted him dead, you should have been enraged. And yet I know you love us because you let us do all this and then gave us yet another chance when he rose again. *Amen.*

Pentecost

Dear Lord,
In the same way that you touched your disciples with the Holy Spirit, kindle your fire within our hearts so that we may be able to accept you as you show yourself to us in our everyday lives – whether it be through friendship, worship or just the peacefulness of prayer. *Amen*.

Dear Lord,
Long ago, you started the church when you sent down your Holy Spirit upon the twelve disciples. Help us to realise that we too can experience the same joy today that they experienced by receiving your most precious gift. We know that you will always be there and all we have to do is call on you. Thank you for this. *Amen*.

Dear Lord,
At this time of Pentecost and at the coming of the Holy Spirit let us celebrate.
You died, you conquered death and you rose again for our salvation.
You filled our hearts with the Holy Spirit, giving confidence to call you Father.
You gave us the chance to teach your word and spread the Christian faith; help us to use this power and not let it slip away. We can then make disciples of all nations, baptising them in your love.
Like Thomas, help us to combat our doubts and have

faith that you will always be with us to the very end. *Amen.*

Lord,
Thank you for sending your Holy Spirit to strengthen, help and guide me. It's so wonderful knowing that a part of you is with me always helping me to come closer to you. *Amen.*

Dear Lord,
Thank you for giving us the strength and power to deal with all situations in life through the power of your Holy Spirit. We pray that just as those early Christians received your Holy Spirit so may we also receive *HIM.* Thank you Lord. *Amen.*

For the Church

Sometimes, Dear God,
Church is unbearable but at other times it's really alive.
Keep the source of this mighty river of Christianity full
of love and welcome. *Amen.*

Dear God,
Thank you for the Church, for the whole lot of friends
we make through it, and for being our friend. *Amen.*

Dear Father,
We pray for strength and unity in the Church throughout
the world, especially in places where other conflicts
hinder its growth and blot out or destroy the message
that we are trying to spread. *Amen.*

Father,
When people see the Church they see bishops in ornate
robes and architectural wonders.
Open their eyes Lord, and let them see your Church, the
living Church, people, millions of people, all over the
world, ordinary people in ordinary places loving one
another. *Amen.*

Dear Father,
Thank you that as well as giving us our natural families
you made us part of your family, the Church, that we

might meet in fellowship and gain encouragement by being with other Christians.
Please help the members of our church to come closer together in unity and understanding. *Amen.*

For the Youth Group

Dear Lord,
Thank you for youth groups. It's great to know that we can meet with other Christians and share our faith together. We praise you Lord. *Amen*.

Dear God,
You have brought many young people together of all nationalities to share your love. Each time we meet our love grows stronger. Be with us in our youth groups and help us to learn and understand your ways. Let our faith ripen in the unity of fellow Christians and let our love for one another grow each day. Help us all to live by your teachings and guide us along the right path. *Amen*.

Dear Lord,
I pray now for our youth group. It is so encouraging to see so many friends enjoying themselves together. Help us to spread your love. Give us strength Lord to teach others your word.
I thank you for the leaders who give up so much of their time for us and I thank you that we are able to meet together freely.
I hope that our group will grow in your Holy Spirit and may your love be shown on all of our faces.
I pray for all the other Christian youth groups in the world.

Help them all to find your love. Shine your light upon us.
Lord, in your name. *Amen.*

Dear God,
We thank you for our youth group. Although we may not be very large, we all take active parts in helping the Church. Help us to know and understand more about you so that we can spread your word to others, particularly people our own age. Help us to make others welcome so that we may become bigger and stronger. Thank you God. *Amen.*

Thank you Lord for the various organisations to which we belong, expecially the Brownies, Guides, Cubs, Scouts and Boys Brigade. Thank you for the people who lead us and put a lot of time and hard work into these activities. May your Holy Spirit guide them in all their preparations.
In Jesus' name. *Amen.*

Father,
Through you our youth group was formed, through your love you have bound us together. We share many wonderful and fulfilling friendships and you give us time to be together and energy to enjoy that time. Thank you for the leaders who help us and encourage us.
    Lord give us the strength to include anyone who is new or lonely, let us be gentle and warm so that they will feel comfortable and a part of our group as we know how important the feeling of being included is. Thank you for the chance to praise you together. *Amen.*

Dear Lord,
We know that you are always with us. When we come together you rejoice. Help our youth group always to renew and reaffirm our commitment to you whenever or wherever we meet. Help us to value the time and friendships we make and guide us so that we may all follow the way to you Lord. *Amen.*

Some Famous Prayers

Lord, make us instruments of your peace.

Where there is hatred, let us sow love;
Where there is injury, pardon;
Where there is discord, union;
Where there is doubt, faith;
Where there is despair, hope;
Where there is darkness, light;
Where there is sadness, joy;

O Divine Master, grant that we may not so much seek
to be consoled as to console;
to be understood as to understand;
to be loved, as to love;
through the love of thy Son who died for us, Jesus
Christ
our Lord. *Amen.*

ST FRANCIS

O God, give us

Serenity to accept what cannot be changed;
Courage to change what should be changed;
And wisdom to distinguish the one from the other;
Through Jesus Christ our Lord. *Amen.*

REINHOLD NIEBUHR

Day by day, dear Lord, of thee
Three things we pray:
To see thee more clearly;
To love thee more dearly;
To follow thee more nearly;
Day by day. *Amen.*

ST RICHARD OF CHICHESTER

Christ has no body now
  on earth but yours.
No hands but yours,
No feet but yours;
Yours are the eyes
  through which is to look out
Christ's compassion to the World;
Yours are the feet
  with which he is
to go about doing good;
Yours are the hands
  with which he is
to bless us now.

ST TERESA OF AVILA

Christ be with me, Christ within me,
Christ behind me, Christ before me,
Christ beside me, Christ to win me,
Christ to comfort and restore me.
Christ beneath me, Christ above me,
Christ in quiet, Christ in danger,
Christ in heart of all that love me,
Christ in mouth of friend and stranger. *Amen.*

ST PATRICK

Teach us, good Lord
To serve thee as thou deservest;
To give and not to count the cost;
To fight and not to heed the wounds;
To toil and not to seek for rest;
To labour and not to ask for any reward,
Save that of knowing that we do thy will. *Amen.*

ST IGNATIUS LOYOLA

O gracious and Holy Father,
Give us wisdom to see thee,
intelligence to understand thee,
diligence to seek thee,
patience to wait for thee,
eyes to behold thee,
a heart to meditate upon thee,
and a life to proclaim thee,
through the power of the Spirit of
Jesus Christ our Lord. *Amen.*

ST BENEDICT

Give us O God:

Thoughts which turn into prayer,
Prayer which turns into love,
Love which turns into deeds. *Amen.*

Eternal God and Father,
you create us by your power
and redeem us by your love:
guide and strengthen us by your Spirit,
that we may give ourselves in love and service
to one another and to you;
through Jesus Christ our Lord. *Amen.*

Our Father in heaven,
hallowed be your name,
your kingdom come,
your will be done,
on earth as in heaven.
Give us today our daily bread.
Forgive us our sins
as we forgive those who sin against us.
Lead us not into temptation
but deliver us from evil.
For the kingdom, the power, and the glory
are yours
now and for ever. *Amen.*

Crowdbreakers

Bob Moffett

A jam-packed book of ideas on what to do with an energetic crowd of teenagers, that will satisfy their appetite for fun, establish trust between group members and effectively communicate the Christian Gospel.

Trade paperback   805139   144 pp

Crowdmakers

Bob Moffett

Bob Moffett uses his imaginative skills in suggesting ways of communicating the Christian Gospel to teenagers. An invaluable resource book full of practical ideas for all youth leaders.

Trade paperback   805880   160 pp

The Sacred Diary of Adrian Plass aged 37¾
Illustrated by Dan Donovan

Adrian Plass

A full-length, side-splitting paperback based on the hilarious diary entries in Christian Family magazine of Adrian Plass, 'an amiable but somewhat inept Christian'. By his own confession, Adrian 'makes many mistakes and is easily confused', but a reassuring sense of belonging to the family of God is the solid, underlying theme. Best-selling Christian book of 1987.

Pocket paperback   014180   160 pp

The Growing Up Pains of Adrian Plass

Adrian Plass

Sacred diarist and TV presenter Adrian Plass tells his *own* story. With a mischievous eye for detail, disarming honesty and irresistible humour, Adrian charts his progress to faith and beyond. Adrian creates an immediate and unforgettable sense of the presence of God in the middle of ordinary life. Previously published under the title, *Join the Company*.

Pocket paperback   013850   160 pp

Working with Teenagers

Nicholas Aiken

Working with Teenagers is at once theoretical
and practical, and sets new and bold targets for
all those involved in youth work. There is a
wealth of useful facts and advice to enable the
youth leader to plan an interesting and varied
programme.

Trade paperback   016493   160 pp

Collected Wisdom for Youth Workers

Edited by Ian Green

A dynamic book packed with useful resource
material for youth workers, featuring
contributions from some outstanding figures
in the field including George Verwer, Clive
Calver and Roger Forster. Foreword by Floyd
McClung.

Trade paperback   016078   160 pp

The Theatrical Tapes
of Leonard Thynn
Illustrated by Dan Donovan

Adrian Plass

Do not miss this final volume of the most successful Christian trilogy ever written!

All the familiar characters from *The Sacred Diary of Adrian Plass* and *The Horizontal Epistles of Andromeda Veal* are taking part in recording sessions to produce Leonard Thynn's extraordinary theatrical tapes. As the fellowship get together in public for the last time they produce a dramatic version of 'Daniel in the Lion's Den', which of course you will never be able to read in the same way again. Wit and humour, tears, laughter and faith sparkle through. A book to relish, enjoy again and again and ideal for giving to all your friends.

Pocket paperback   018755   142 pp